PRAISE FOR

"*Stonechat* is a remarkable book, flu
connected to family and a New Eng
Mary Elder Jacobsen carefully shapes each poem to its subject, the poems soaring with an easy, unforced lyricism, as in 'Postcards from a Stack Tied Up with Twine,' a sonnet sequence addressed to her late father. When she writes, 'I know the rare particulars of this vast and intimate brilliance— / the *now* of us—won't ever, in our lifetime, come my way again,' we believe her. Over and over, these beautiful poems confirm the singularity of Jacobsen's experience."

—Elizabeth Spires, author of *A Memory of the Future*

"In poem after poem, Mary Elder Jacobsen delights her reader with a vision, upended: the newborn's bath becomes the dying father's; the bees we keep *keep us*. 'I have always loved the word *reflection*,' she admits, and her work does, beautifully, mirror, but it also sees *in*, with surprising, compassionate depths. Like water finding its basin (of course Jacobsen lives on a lake!), the poems form, as ode, villanelle, sonnet—each holding but not containing the perfect 'punctuated surface that reflects the world she breathes.'"

—Jody Gladding, author of *I entered without words*

"In poem after poem in *Stonechat,* Mary Elder Jacobsen maintains an Edenic wonder at the natural world with a verbal music that flows with internal rhymes, alliteration, and cascading lyrical lines. Charged with unslaked enthusiasm for her subjects, the poet sustains riveting attention to her immense particulars that add up to a poetic sum that is greater than the whole of her subjects and conceits by virtue of their verbal magic in which they continue to 'sing' anew each time they're read or heard."

—Chard deNiord, Poet Laureate of Vermont (2015–2019)

"I have been a fan of Mary Elder Jacobsen's incisive and precise poems for many years now. From the opening sequence of *Stonechat*, it's evident that her debut collection is a culmination of countless hours of devotion to craft and love for the actual world. Jacobsen makes the everyday shimmer with life, so that a simple oyster becomes 'the ark where life resides… tiny cradle, bearer of treasure.' Even Queen Anne's lace, in her hands, becomes a 'perennial herd' with 'white tufted tails' hiding in a meadow made sacred by this poet's close attention, her immense command of language and form."

—James Crews, author of *Unlocking the Heart: Writing for Mindfulness, Creativity, and Self-Compassion*

"Jacobsen's strong, clear poems make an accidental almanac for loving the passage of days. The finely tuned music reenacts how 'the bees, the bees, left us / amazed under plum trees.' Other poems have such indelible images they become a sheaf of 'favorite Polaroid[s]…your face a flower tipping toward the sun.' Even as she deploys a variety of poetic forms with playful excellence—a crown of sonnets, ghazal, villanelle, ekphrastic—anyone could wander into this work and find a resonant sentiment. The collection as a whole encompasses, investigates, and celebrates Ceres' vicinity—as Jacobsen invokes both the goddess of grain and the harvest by including a pasture's worth of plants in her poems—among them: Queen Anne's lace, sumac, hawthorn, goldenrod, even 'fresh-shucked corn stacked nearly too high.' As well, Jacobsen pays homage to the actual statue atop the Vermont State House dome, a dozen miles from her dooryard, and the landscape basking between: a swath of dirt roads, forests, lakes and cow pastures, and the family and friends she's made within this lush geography. Across the volume, the poet's sustained gaze at motherhood, daughterhood, a cherished husband and son, as well as a deep understanding of home allows readers 'the rare particulars' of Jacobsen's 'intimate brilliance.' This full-hearted collection is the perfect book to steep in and savor throughout seasons, but especially in the 'long stretches of chill and dark and damp.'"

—Julia Shipley, award-winning journalist and poet, author of *The Academy of Hay*

"I hardly know where to begin—with Jacobsen's studious and precise eye? her deft musicality? her formal inventiveness? with the way these poems enact deep love for family and the natural world? The poems in Mary Elder Jacobsen's Stonechat rove between intimacies, seeing with an eye both human and mythic, their gaze cutting across a full life and a secluded patch of land that seems, at the same time, as big as the world. These poems sing and dig. I was sideswiped by 'Sorting the Dark from the Light,' a poem about washing a mother's 'last nightgown'—the way this poem treads into duality, building a waltz between the living and the dead, ending 'We're waltzing, not weeping. / Stop weeping, we're waltzing.'"

—Kerrin McCadden, author of *American Wake*

Stonechat

poems

Mary Elder Jacobsen

Montpelier, VT

Stonechat copyright 2023 ©Mary Elder Jacobsen
All Rights Reserved.

Release Date: April 9, 2024

Printed in the USA.

Published by Rootstock Publishing
an imprint of Ziggy Media LLC
Montpelier, Vermont 05602
info@rootstockpublishing.com
www.rootstockpublishing.com

Softcover ISBN: 978-1-57869-168-5
eBook ISBN: 978-1-57869-171-5
Library of Congress Number: 2023952316

Cover Art: "Entita i Topp" ("Marshtit on top"), 1995, woodcut by Kristina Anshelm, collection of the author's family, used with permission. Image scan by Linda Mirabile, RavenMark.

Book design by Eddie Vincent, ENC Graphics Services.

Author photo by E. E. Jacobsen.

No part of this book may be reproduced or transmitted in any form or by any means, electronic or mechanical, including photocopying, recording, or by an information storage and retrieval system—except by a member of the press or a reviewer who may quote brief passages for a review in a magazine or newspaper—without permission in writing.

To request permissions or reach the author, please see the contact page at www.maryelderjacobsen.com.

For my animal family—
kin, kind friends, and kindred spirits all,
both wild and domestic.

Contents

Sleepwalker	1
Reflection	2
Water Views	3
Diptych: Boathouse in Autumn Rain	4
I, Caddisfly	6
This Be the Oyster	7
Pondweed	8
Blue	9
White Space & Ink: An Erasure	10
Weaverbird	11
Wild in the Meadow	13
The Red This Fall	14
Between Here and There	15
After the Floods	16
On Waking	17
Above the Fold	18
The Sky Breaks and You're on Your Own	19
Dragonfly	20
Come Home	21
Sponge Bath	23
Stonechat	25
This Is Not a Poem	26
The Dream	27
Ode to Ceres and Her Golden Dome	28
In Some Random Corner	29
While I Watched 100 Buttons Being Carefully Counted Out for Kindergarten Homework	30
As the Early Sun Tiptoes around the House	31
Taking a Walk before My Son's 18th Birthday	33
Child	34
Birthdays Like Chanterelles in Golden Light	35

Wiping Dust from the *Atlas of Human Anatomy* in the Used Bookshop	36
How to Grow a Sonnet	37
Slice of Morning	38
How a Sonnet Wakes Up	39
Squirrel	40
Summer Cottage	41
Sonnet for Stick Season	42
Another Hole This Winter	43
Encyclopedias	44
Postcards from a Stack Tied Up with Twine	45
Animal Stories	49
En Plein Air	51
Beekeeping	52
Some Curse, Some Sing	53
Shadows	55
Notes from Woods Edge	56
Fibonacci Blues	57
Orion	58
The Pleiades	59
Water Lily	60
Cochlear	61
Sorrow Ghazal	62
Hourglass	64
Watchmaker	65
Out on the Lake in Our Old Canoe	66
Why I Still Write	67
The Sea of Poetry	69
Sorting the Dark from the Light	71
Notes	75
Acknowledgments	77
Gratitude	79

♦

/ˈstōnˌCHat/ noun

a small Old World songbird of the thrush subfamily, having bold markings and a call that sounds like two stones being knocked together.

♦

*The grouse lets us watch
as she eats the fall apples
raising our spirits*

—R.B.E.

♦

*When we look we are in grief,
and also in gratitude for the beauty of the world.
Grief and gratitude, what other responses can we possibly have to life?*

—Mary Ruefle

♦

Sleepwalker

after the woodcut "Sömngångaren"
by Swedish printmaker Kristina Anshelm

Silver-sharp blade up against the inky night,
the crescent moon's razor shaves a narrow swath
of stubbled grass much brighter than the rest,
and like a velvet aisle on which a bride has trod,
this moonlit stretch of field is hers and hers
alone. Her simple dress is more akin to shift
than nuptial gown. It is the night she wears
and weds, and in a trance of dark and light
she moves away toward waking and all married is.

Reflection

I have always loved the word *reflection*—

the way it sneaks up from behind at different angles,
shows off in the polished-chrome wing mirrors
of some guy's prized '55 Thunderbird, preening in a bevy
of vintage cars parked on Nichols Field; the way it dangles
in pearly luster, in the teardrop earrings my neighbor wears;
the way it both recedes and comes in close to face you
like the supermoon, or those other random, skewed views—
domestic interiors lost in orbit inside antique convex mirrors.
I love how it comes to play with sunlight on water,
like an enviable toddler dancing freely with no one
but himself; how it can be visible—image refraction—
or audible—the way a wild echo will luff and taper
as the loons call back and forth across the lake,
deflecting their songs of hunger, lust, labor, distress,
rapture, success; how the fledgling loon, taken aback
with it, catches sight of her upside-down-self
and laughs, coos her muted hoot, then trails along
in the rippling tremolo of her mother's wake.
For the pause it gives—
                              for pausing's sake;
for its open invite to anyone;
                              for its *hey, wait, look*—
I have always loved the word *reflection*.

Water Views

Upside down
the hillside
whispers blue,
green, water—
It ripples
its echo
oh oh oh
kissing shore
and dissolves
by and by
and dissolves
kissing shore
oh oh oh
its echo,
it ripples
green, water,
whispers blue
the hillside
downside up.

Diptych: Boathouse in Autumn Rain

As the punctuated surface reflects the world she breathes,
her glance flitting from stippled lake to scribbled page,
all day the writer inside writes to the same hypnotic air—
rainfall's percussive snare riffing from ridge to eaves,
a liquid song rung from metal hulls, from stern to bow,
from bright overturned boats in rows like chromatic bells
all untethered and glinting back toward the boathouse door,
toward daydreams of plying the lake like splashing oars,
a steady downbeat waking the watery view—*beat, beat, beat*—
through the day's sleepy stillness, the blurry scrim of rain,
sticks and needle brushes working the old tin roof,
still-lit tamaracks flashing their tiny flecks of golden bling,
with only a few proud trees hanging on late, even the faintest
handfuls giving in, tired oaks fling their waterlogged confetti
as wet November's heavy sigh nearly drowns the sky, for hours
upon hours, muffling the rustling chatter of leaves. Still,
something else stirs, what's here in the drone on drone?
Gray rain, gray squirrel, gray bird—what's left, what else?

*For my animal family—
kin, kind friends, and kindred spirits all,
both wild and domestic.*

Gray rain, gray squirrel, gray bird—what's left, what else?
Something else stirs, what's here in the drone on drone
upon hours muffling the rustling chatter of leaves *still*
as wet November's heavy sigh nearly drowns the sky? For hours,
handfuls giving in, tired oaks fling their waterlogged confetti.
With only a few proud trees hanging on late, even the faintest
still-lit tamaracks flashing their tiny flecks of golden bling—
sticks and needle brushes working the old tin roof.
Through the day's sleepy stillness, the blurry scrim of rain,
a steady downbeat waking the watery view—*beat, beat, beat*—
toward daydreams of plying the lake like splashing oars,
all untethered, and glinting back toward the boathouse door,
from bright overturned boats in rows like chromatic bells,
a liquid song rung from metal hulls from stern to bow,
rainfall's percussive snare riffing from ridge to eaves—
All day the writer inside writes to the same hypnotic air,
her glance flitting from stippled lake to scribbled page
as the punctuated surface reflects the world she breathes.

I, Caddisfly

If you can say a piece of paper is a
leaf,
or say that pages of a book are
leaves,
so might I say that papier-mâché is
innately, and to wit, my
oeuvre.
So too, I say: No mere mud dauber am I—
I, caddisfly—
which is to say, the realm I'm in
remains upon and under waves, where wavering
I weave
more bit by bit as artisan
to build my world of spit and leaf
from self and lake
whose underwater weeds I moistly masticate
as I see fit, which is to say, in truth,
intuit, and lately
(mostly lost in all absorption),
in fits and in spurts,
I hiccup into view
these words of *me*
to house the world of I—
I, caddisfly.

This Be the Oyster

This be the cup, brimming fathoms of nectar
This, the well that flows from forever

This be the saltcellar, trencher of tears,
and also the teardrop, stone-wept from ocean

This be the stone, lost among cairns,
and there, another, hidden in middens

This be the hull that casts off its seed—
thus grows the reef, encrusted with life—

This, ancient vessel, anchored to reef,
This be the ark where life resides

and this, tiny cradle, bearer of treasure,
This be the oyster, slow-rocked by tides.

Pondweed

The grass is greener under-
water. I've grown green with envy over every under-
water weed, so long and thinly, loved and lively, glint and greenly
under-
water. Fluidly, movingly under-
water. Leave me, grow me, willowy green me under-
water. Ebb and billow me. Lap and please me. Leave me be thee under-
water. O ribbon me, oh ravel me. Oh under-
water's where un-
done I've long become have gone and go under
spells and lo how soon am over-
whelmed by deep by shallow
waters all and in whose realms I'll gladly dwell, all unhoused and
under-
water. Take me under,
water me there, make me pondweed under-
water, un-
dulate me under-
water.

Blue

Blue spilled out
and soaked the world,
stained the sky and broke.

Like pieces of Blue Willow china
it fell or like glaze it flowed,
thread through the eye of a needle,
blue in the space of a flame,
the border of island and cloud,
the lip of a cup or the dead.

Blue are the fingers that knead
coastlines whose fingers are jetties.

Blue shakes free from hands that hold
a vessel that pours to the ground
shattered shards and spray that fly
back up into air blue splinters
legs of a heron
needles of spruce
the almighty feathers
of blue jays.

WHITE SPACE & INK: AN ERASURE

*Paper opened up
a whole new world, images
transferred to paper—*

*a simple process:
dampened paper over stone
brushed to mold itself.*

*In scroll form—sacred
words, images, deities
would come to be known—*

*all cut in relief,
cut on the same block of wood
then coated with ink,*

*and paper was pressed
against the surface. After?*

The paper lifted off...

Weaverbird

Epithalamium, for R.

A breeze floats through this clearing. Below,
the brook babbles, washing the land
with its own blessing. Where does one begin,
the other end? The sound of wind
and water are one, as if woven.

Today even shadow and light are one,
thread through the woods' edge in a tapestry
that unfolds around us, along with song—
bird, brook, breeze—the voices of joyful company.
How have we come together? Effortlessly

as brook flows into brook, creating a third
whose waters are no longer two but one?
Or was I drawn to you like the weaverbird—?
the weaverbird whose mate attracts her
by the nest he builds *before* she's chosen him.

How deftly he weaves leaf into branch upon branch
into leaf until what grows before her she knows
will be her home. How lucky the weaverbird.
She thinks, "But what have I to show you
who I am, have been, will be?" He goes

about his love's labor, no audible reply,
until the intricate layerings of his love
have shown her: The answer to her is him,
and to him is her. In clear blue sky
she alights upon his branch, her trills spiraling above—

I choose you, sings the weaverbird.
Oh yes, and yes again! I do, I do, I do.

Wild in the Meadow

How all at once they twitch white tufted tails
and then, windblown, bend down, now nearly hidden,
for a minute lost in chest-high switchgrass,
in gusts of wind, summer's musky air, dusk—

I've grown to think each year of this as ours,
this perennial herd, neither ruminant nor
ungulate this herd, and yet how like them—
to keep returning, to let me witness how
in our field they stretch and nudge and nose
about, rise up, grow wild, grow tame, hold still,
lie down again, and every time my surprise
is less what *they* are not or are than who
I am / become / will be among them, how knowing
from discerning this is to watch myself, grown
lost in this to-do of Queen Anne's lace,
to stand again, startled here by every breath,
to stare and stare, to wait and see each year
how they've come back, how wild, how they scatter.

THE RED THIS FALL

It is the red I won't forget. The fire-
engine red of taillights blinking, the road
pulsing as leaf peepers braked for fall, high-
bush cranberries, their ruby-reds aglow,

that shiny, idled, stop-sign-red sports car,
a couple snapping selfies next to flame-red
leaves. My son's face, flushed from rushing upstairs
to find me writing by the window. I'd heard
the door slam shut. *Mom*, his mouth quivering,
The baby loon is dead.
                      I won't forget it,
the red that caught his eye while he was paddling,
the red, on shore, that *wasn't* someone's forgotten
towel but, as he grew near, was clear: the winged
young life undone, blood-red, heart pierced open.

Between Here and There

North Calais, Vermont
February 2022

Between the sun and me: more than
90 million miles. Between
Ukraine and me: a full seven
hours. Between windows, the hope
chest that my father built by hand
for me. Inside: decades, decades
of memories. Across distance
and time, how struck I am by this
one sun, how it can warm my cheek,
right *here*, and also glisten, *there*,
on tear-stricken cheeks of children
roused from bed, fleeing with mothers
on foot, feels like forever, hands
clasped, leaving their fathers behind
to help the heroes, to save their homes.

After the Floods

Where went the sky that emptied itself into the green mountains
Who moved the mountains that emptied themselves into the rivers

Fast flowed the rivers that emptied themselves into the roads
Where be the roads that emptied themselves of black tar

Of rock of earth of culvert of bridge span and now dam
Into the cellars stairwells hidey-holes oh god the bric-a-brac

All through the mudrooms dining rooms living rooms rec rooms
Here heave the homes filled up fed-up flooded-up

Wrecked with mud with roads with rivers with mountains
Inside inside inside the houses themselves

Breaching retching reaching end over end
Lost and found a posted sign still pinned up

Outside everyone looking left looking right
Looking up looking down each dwelling emptied

Inside out out out onto the streets lost utterly
Lost who has seen has anyone seen the sky
Where went oh my my dear parents' clear blue sky?

On Waking

Before you get all tangled up in today's confusion
or worry just where to begin amid the chaos, hush—
let the first thoughts of the morning be your own.

Forget the daily news, leave those headlines alone.
Wake up slowly, splash your face, find your hairbrush,
before you get all tangled up. In dawn's confusion,

it's crazy how we lose sight of things. One by one—
busy, busy—we race past ourselves. Whatever, don't rush.
Let the first thoughts of the morning be your own.

Let yourself pause, let the quiet come. You're okay, alone
with the breeze, the gray squirrel, the thrush in the cranberry bush.
Before you get all tangled up in the day's confusion,

picture yourself by a window, on the outside looking in,
like that small fox just scampering out of the brush—
and let the first thoughts of the morning be your own.

Then watch as you and the path you're on become one,
weaving your way forward, clear and refreshed.
Before you get all tangled up in the day's confusion
let the first thoughts of the morning be your own.

Above the Fold

after a photo by Jeb Wallace-Brodeur in the
Barre-Montpelier Times Argus

A stroller in front of her, a ribbon of toddlers
tied on behind her, the caregiver takes small steps
along Montpelier's salted sidewalks, front yards
of snow melting to her left, paved roads kept
plowed, running like rivers, to her right.
January thaw. The sun shines. She believes
in getting out each day, believes spring might
be just around the next corner, believes
in *safety first*. The children believe in *her*,
believe in snacks, believe in naps, believe
in walking field trips to see frozen water-
falls, believe in play, believe in wearing
boots to keep feet dry, mittens to keep hands
warm, and winter hats as orange as traffic
cones to keep being seen.
                              Reader, believe in *this*,
spread the news, this world, it still has good in it.

The Sky Breaks and You're on Your Own

After a long spell of no hope
for fresh snow, there comes a sudden
squall. All night long the dark
darkens with it. When day breaks,
the sky blues, and you're stepping out
into early morning. You don't expect
to be seen. In black muck boots,
rumpled robe, holey fleece, you heft
the oversized shovel and ask yourself
if you can handle it all alone.
Load by doable load you move
this new world from here to there
across the old back road. You hear
what sound? Your neighbor shifting gears.
He slows. Says *Hello*. Speaks
your name. Asks if he can help
Push this all away? His open window
lets you see him clearly. Young,
too-young widowed. You remember
his wife's name before his own.
How long has it been, you wonder.
There, in his big pickup with its huge
plow, he looks small. You both know
some cliché weather jokes. He smiles
small smiles. *Touch his shoulder*
your reflex says. *I'm so sorry*
your mouth says. *I can't not say
something*—your heart says—*about
Carolyn.* The air completely stills.
This grief is deep. It reaches his eyes.

Dragonfly

Late morning, one settles down on a leaf afloat,
plying his chain-mail oars, his little raft a fragile boat.

My father would say *darner* where I saw "dragonfly."
Who knows any longer what a darner is? Time flies.

Late afternoon, Lake's hem unraveling, Sun squints
toward dusk—leaning in to finish her day's stitches.

Evening now, I listen to one upstairs window closing,
as I turn to open up another, letting a Luna moth go,

then watch as my father, grown tired, senses the fading
light above the fabric knee patch he's been sewing.

Handing me his spool and needle, he smiles just to see
how easily I swim his thread through the oh-so-tiny eye.

Come Home

At a loss, my father unlatches the old farmhouse door,
not really there, believes he glimpses his hen house, hears
its cockeyed hinges, knows that humus air, and more.
But his childhood home lies miles, years from here.

When my mother sees him staring off, she wonders
where he's gone, and soon he returns to find her—
scratching her nib on paper, counting out pips she pours
from orange bottles. Roaming further, he remembers paper

ribbons, candy buttons, how they could take his frown away,
yet now, how his favorite foods have no taste, how old songs
keep coming back to stay, and stay, how his body betrays
him, his mind fails him, how it's all become so tiring.

When my mother sees him fading, she calls for her chicks
to come. *Cluck, cluck, cluck,* she sings. Trembling,
her wings swoop out, then in. How she aches and aches
to cradle more than air, already half-embracing

us not yet there, until her small brood flies in again
from all directions... Our shadows flit about her feet
as her fingers meet, her hands clutch, her arms arcing around
the space we're in, a circling path rejoined, complete,

as in some playground game of aggies—an outline drawn
by a child's hand, a giant *O* on clean-swept ground,
where jewel-like marbles, all together and all alone,
swirl within the bleary ring, then whirl beyond

its bounds. When none remain, the game is done.
The children playing on their knees have lost their sun—

Evening's come. The porch light glows with day grown dim
and beckons to the boy inside the man, *Come home, come home.*

Sponge Bath

I

At first, to let him know I'm here,
I start with song, a kind of coo,
or croon. My voice breaks,
morning waking into lullaby.
I test the water at my wrist,
here, the bare pulse point.
Not hot. Not cold. Just warm.
I dip the soft infant cloth into
the wash basin, swish, and squeeze.
Damp, not dripping. I bring
some order to our routine, begin
with crown, brow, temples.
Traveling the topography
of the face—ears, eyes,
mouth, nose—all our animal
pathways, I grow humbled
by the whole of us, this space
I find myself within, caring for
another being, my newborn
at home, only a few days old,
a kind of gift that overwhelms,
to know we've only just begun
to say hello.

II

At first, to let him know I'm here,
I start with song, a kind of coo,
or croon. My voice breaks,
morning waking into lullaby.

I test the water at my wrist,
here, the bare pulse point,
make sure it's warm, just right.
I dip the soft terry washcloth into
the basin, swish, and squeeze.
Damp, not dripping. I bring
some order to our routine, begin
with crown, brow, temples.
Traveling the topography
of the face—all the tender
pathways to sound, sight,
taste, smell, I've grown humbled
by the whole of us, the space
I'm standing in, caring for
this other being, my father only
days from passing, here at home,
a strange kind of gift. It overwhelms,
to know we've only just begun
to say goodbye.

Stonechat

Who first thought to name it?
Who first heard its cry?

Before she heard the Stonechat
did she stoop at river's edge,
the weight of an infant pack heavy
on her back, her blistered feet
blessed by the water's foaming eddies?
Did she ask what sort of pebbles fall
that they may sound like birds singing?

When she first heard the Stonechat
did she hear the rhythmic whisper
her broom sang into air, moving
its patterns across the dirt floor?
Did she pause long enough to notice
the design her body and broom had wrought
out of the dry earth, the straw-combed
hearth at her feet, the way the ribbed dirt
lay like a tablet before her? Perhaps
it was then that she squatted down
to trace her name in the blankness, then
when she called the lines her own,
connected sound to sight and heard
again the falling pebbles, their music
drawing her eye to an open window
through which she saw, on a wavering branch,
small and copper-breasted amid white flowers
and dark berries, the song's true source
to which she listened, then wrote beside her name:
Stonechat, Stonechat, Stonechat.

This Is Not a Poem

just a list, for R.

This is not a poem, it's just a list
in fourteen lines, some things I love knowing
because you're in this life with me—the gist
of you that makes me smile—like your nose,
all yellow with pollen after you've been sniffing
flowers in our garden; like your eyes, that blue
sky mirrored in them, the lake's morning mist,
herons, kingfishers, vireos; joys you've brought me to,
like blue-eyed grass, woodland mosses, Aurora
Borealis; like us, paddling on clear waters;
like lake swims, a.m. & p.m., full moon in our mirror,
the call and splash of loons; like making the ordinary
life extraordinary; like never getting over
the gift of every kiss, each day, another hour.

The Dream

after the painting "Dream" (1945) by Marc Chagall

I'm done with "love"—*I think I'll take a nap,*
or that, at least, is what I'd told myself,
but then I fell into the deepest sleep
and dreamed *you* there. I was beside myself
with joy—how to say?... Oh, *floating on air*—
as if we two dwelled within a miracle
wherein I visioned all that I hold dear,
the city, the Seine, Paris!, her Eiffel
Tower, that azure sky, the full moon a kind
of halo holding us as you held me—
plus your bouquet—cottage roses, lupines,
what else? I heard a fiddler's tunes, the beat
of drums? a dancer's clogs? or horses' hooves?
Oh Love, *my heart* it was, all woke for you!

Ode to Ceres and Her Golden Dome

> "Montpelier's 'golden dome' to get a makeover"
> —*News story headline, WCAX, Montpelier, Vermont*

> "We believe it's been regilded ten times in the last century, and it started in 1906… Gilding domes, it turns out, is not something that has changed all that much."
> —*David Schütz, Vermont State Curator*

Before the re-gilders can touch up the dome—
to match the gold that Ceres stands upon,
they'll have to find the just-right leaf, in sheen
and tone, the glint and hue of hillsides, Autumn
afternoons, old pastures guilty with goldenrod
or proud with grain, Monet's deft touch, end-of-summer
brushwork, mounded haystacks, and oh, right here,
that shimmering hour when tucked-in farms nod
to dusk as sun bends down to kiss Vermont,
the light gilding acres and acres of burnished wheat,
timothy, rye, even the yellow-gold surprise
of fresh-shucked corn stacked nearly too high,
up on kitchen tables, by eager children who must wait—
bright bits of corn silk clinging to their blue dungarees.

In Some Random Corner

Sometimes I wonder if God could be a spider
just hanging out in a random corner somewhere,
maybe in some child's bedroom, there long before
the child ever laid eyes on it, just over there
doing its spider thing, doing its God thing.
Sometimes I wonder why I think this way—
hanging out here in some random corner all day—
but before long I'm back to the spider weaving,
back to that web hanging up there in the corner,
back to the child—boy or girl, doesn't matter.
Anyway, I should get back now to the wondering,
to hanging out in a random corner somewhere,
to the child inside, watching the God-spider,
awake, wide-eyed, held rapt by the weaving.

While I Watched 100 Buttons Being Carefully Counted Out for Kindergarten Homework

I never told our kindergartner
about the buttons lost to ardor
but kept the stories rated G
and focused on the ABCs,
the 123s, the primaries,
just yellow, red, and blue to start,
skipped the parts that get learned later,
how what we know gets all stirred up—
enchantment mixing in a cup—
to make some orange, sunset bright,
and green, for fresh-mown grass that's lush
enough for tumbling, head over
heels, kissed with dew, toward breathless dusks,
and sweet purple, shades of midnight
bodies ripened beneath the moon,
small love bites in the afterglow,
every single button undone.

As the Early Sun Tiptoes around the House

I dig out my parents' old gardening tools,
unearthing cold air from the pockets of their canvas tote,
tote freed from our still-chilled shed, its doorway opened up,
its insides all alit. Morning's long-angled light stretches,
blinks, catches on blades of dew-wet grass, on blades
of grass shears, pitchfork tines, edge of hoe, trowel scoop—

all glint, all patina-polished—and everywhere else
my joys crop up: new shoots, old perennials, scents of soil,
of creek overrun, of new winter rye. I even spy grass patches
already undone where the dog has gone, dug, buried
and unburied the blue, the orange, the yellow ball like sun—
Where *has* the green been hiding? Snow cover gone,

long-lost fetching balls pop up like crocuses across the lawn.
The garden returning, I've promised myself this early hour
of relearning it. The season changing, it's warm enough
to get down on my bare knees, the way my mother would,
and work with bare hands, ungloved, as my father would,
to move close in, eyes alert, to not miss any new growth.

It's a start, at least, I tell myself. I'll take the passed-down,
these hand-me-downs, what's handheld for just an hour any day
in this place, where on all roving fours I make my way
around our home's foundation to groom the silken strands
of grass, like sleep-tousled hair. I'll leave the wind-sown,
the self-sown, the volunteers I cannot bear to clear: columbine,

forget-me-not, and fern, plus wild-running, soon-to-flower
strawberries our freckled ten-year-old will hunt in June.
Tired white winter behind us, it's hard now to weed
out anything green, to not revere every single sprouting seed

or the magic spell cast upon each just to get this far.
As soon as the early sun tiptoes around the house,

this ink-black space between our old stone steps
will blink with shy, sun-seeking garters
who'll fast outgrow their sleep-crannied hideaways,
their bright oval heads glistening like wet river
stones, their lithe bodies branching out like twigs,
rain-dark and scattered over the granite stairs,

where last year's snake skins, left behind, still flutter
like tiny windbreakers cast off on a playground fence.
The screen door lets me hear our son begin to wake
and stir. Too soon, he'll stretch to his full length, bask
in the day's growing light, wriggle toward wonder,
and leave behind the sloughed skin of his childhood lair.

Taking a Walk before My Son's 18th Birthday

for E.

Not too far from home, I spotted a painted turtle
toddling along, heading across the dirt road.
So I paused there in the hush and just stood still,
so I could watch, and held the dog back on his lead.
When I heard an engine louden along the bend,
then rev uphill behind me, I shifted a little,
worried a bit, then moved myself over and waved,
flagging down the sky-blue pickup with its gravelly rumble,
until the driver, with his lowered window, finally slowed
to a stop, his eyebrows raised, looking quizzical.
So I pointed out the small pedestrian in the road
and the old man gave me a nod, cranked his wheel,
and curved around us, leaving behind the steady turtle—
who made it—and me, still mesmerized by a moving shell.

Child

How you've grown, child
of mine—pearl from my oyster,
you sparkle like snow.

Birthdays Like Chanterelles in Golden Light

for a friend, on turning 70

Some days, they crop up right in front of you.
Easy. Quick. Done. And once you find one, *there*,
and luck is with you, *here*, another one pops into view.
You just can't help but move toward where they are.
Some days, the foraging bewilders you—
the uphill trudge, the path unclear, dried leaves
of seasons past like waves you're wading through.
But then you navigate between the old-growth trees
and make your way toward undiscovered treasure,
where northern evergreens have raised their needles up
to stitch the treetops and blue sky together
to knit a shawl of open weave that lights *you* up,
and all at once, you see the search for what it is—
a chance to find yourself, aglow, in old familiar woods.

Wiping Dust from the *Atlas of Human Anatomy* in the Used Bookshop

Obsessing over topographical studies on yellowed
pages—antique blueprints of the human condition,
I spot hair-thin arrows, blood-red superscripts, scrawled
annotations—scratched out by some learned profession.

I take in copious marginalia (re: muscles, organs,
and skeletal structure). I notice no notes taken,
no inked-in ovations, no key to the complex—humans'
romantic circulation. I see emotion forgotten.

I crave a newer edition that shows more heart; shows
our pulse, breath, blood; shows all the pressures
flowing within us, how our sensibilities can slow
or quicken in relation to the varying measures
of noxious or nutritious words fed through the ears,
morsel by morsel, straight to the maw of the heart.

How to Grow a Sonnet

Be.
Begin.
Bulb, pod, seed.
Begin as one
wee thing. Start out fresh,
fecund, firmly planted—
grounded. Nestle and nourish
your root in the deep-down seedbed.
Soak up, soak up—Quench your greening thirst.
Feed your every hunger, your zoetic
and poetic selves—until, so filled, you burst
forth, uncurl your little sprout, stretch out your live wick
of words, emerging toward the light a strong slender stem
that branches leaf by leaf and at the end erupts—*full bloom.*

Slice of Morning

I'm waking to a sky
dark as chocolate ganache
swirled by the great baker,
her sparkly spatula,
her flourish of icing,
between bright coconut-
fluff layers of snow days
she's stacked up one by one,
yesterday then today,
and soon I remember
the slice of cake sent home
after last night's party
and I'm up like the sun,
first to rise out of bed
down the dim-lit stairwell
followed by the dog, star
of our world. How is it
he can beg shamelessly
for more? His bowl is full.
We are not unalike
after all. Let me slice
this last piece of sweet cake
in half and leave the rest.
Let me keep wanting more.

How a Sonnet Wakes Up

Ears
flinch (*Damn*
those hammers—
at dawn—again!),
then spring to and call
the rest: "Up and at 'em!"
Nose starts, stretches, yawns, and feels
a touch of coffee, bacon, rain.
Skin blinks, rubs sleep-crumbs away, takes in
the view—soft sheets, warm sun, a loved one's flushed
cheek. Tongue roves around in the dark, following
the ridge of gum and tooth, soon finds the roof, then turns
to wander more, not too much, still feeling somewhat hushed.
Thirsty, Eye gulps down the big glass of world by the window.

Squirrel

Scampering scampering, I am I am
an ampersand you track on snow
and and and and
back and forth & to and fro
I come I go, I come I go

Summer Cottage

I'm halfway through a day
that began like a gift
in a blue china eggcup
set on the table before me
by my grandma at the shore
always awake before sunup
always beginning it for me
her soft tap-tap-tapping
her careful cracking to open
what seemed a rare jewel box
how she raised its little lid
let me peek past the edge
let me see the whole horizon
orbiting the yolk-yellow sun
how brightly it would glisten
hovering there just for me.

Sonnet for Stick Season

Trees
minus
leaves.
Us—

sans
gardens,
sans
sun—

grown
grayer
toward
winter.
Wait, don't
wait.

Another Hole This Winter

It's hard to focus on the far-away
ice fishermen, so small, like ants with augers.
They've pitched their shanty. To keep warm, they sway
this way and that in a tight huddle near
their fishing hole, their circle of faces
reflected in the cut-out lake. Now they wait.
Someone will say something. Others will take
their time to speak. They can see their breath. Today's
sharp air is hard to bear. I shiver for them.
Next village over, same sort of scene. But
not. The cemetery road's high snow berm
has been trekked across and a fresh hole dug
in the frozen graveyard. Grieving cold, the huddled
men kick at dirt clods, heads bowed, and search for words.

Encyclopedias

Midway through our guided tour of the Athenaeum,
the silver-haired docent in the Rare Books Room pauses—
There, a complete set, she whispers. (Mum's the word.)
We see them, stock-still, side by side in sisterhood, each reliant
upon the next in line, such faithful aides in their uniform grays
fading at attention. All queued up, like vertebrae, defiant
once against aging, they've grown brittle, with the decades
bearing down, the whole row now bowed like the arcing
spine of someone's dear yet diminished grandmother.

Postcards from a Stack Tied Up with Twine

for my father
R.B.E. (1929–2001)

I

I've got a stack of blank postcards
and I'll be writing to you soon.
I picked them up in town. Both sides
are blank. There's room for words on one
and room for art on the other—
all just waiting to be filled in
so I can send them off to wherever
you are. How long, now, has it been?
I'll save some change on stamps. It all
adds up. The weight of losing you,
whole decades now, the things I'd call
to say to you but can't and so
I write. We said, I remember,
we'd stay in touch. Wish you were here.

II

O Stay-in-touch… O Wish-you-were-
here… O *Hugs-and-kisses*… O *Sending-
love*… O *Weekend-sunny-and-clear*…
Here though, it's mostly cloudy, tending
toward gray, drizzle, more rain. And so
I scribble again. (O *Tears-run-down-
my-window-panes*.) These words I wrote
are mine, but aren't they anyone's?
Clichés preserved in ink, in dust,
on backsides of antique postcards

I've found in vintage shops, all lost
in thought, perfect script, loving words,
news from afar, warm wishes,
X's & O's. Hope you can read this.

III

X's & O's. Hope you can read this.
I'm dabbling again in pen and ink,
remembering the arc and swish
of ABCs in that beginner's book
you gave me when I turned fourteen.
"Your sense of beauty is a joy
to all of us—" you had written on
page one, "May it continue to grow
with you." The author's last name,
Angel, became a talisman to me,
her *Art of Calligraphy* like some
spirit guide hovering beside me.
Everywhere, I'm blessed by gifts of yours.
It's hard sometimes to form the words.

IV

It's more than I can put in words.
I wish that you could see the view
from my window: Toward the dirt road,
an old stone wall, plum trees, a few
apple, heaving and letting go,
the ground beneath a carpet of
windfall, beyond ripe, the scent blowing
everywhere. And there's our small dog
you never got to know, there under
the hammock where your grandson reads,
floating on air between the paper

birch and crabapple trees. You loved
him so at three. We never guessed
then how much life you'd end up missing.

V

How much of life we never did miss.
Can you recall that tall, tall tree,
its tip so high above the rest
a few yards over? How you, me,
mom—all of us—loved to focus
on its spirelike branch where we'd see
that mockingbird perched. So raucous!
He'd twitch his tail, he'd fuss, he'd preen,
then pitch his voice—a finely tuned
ventriloquist who mimicked cat's
meow, bird's song, crow's caw. One
more June presence we'd raise our glasses
to. How you praised all God's creatures.
I'm keeping notes to remind us.

VI

I'm keeping notes. Reminder lists.
Blues and more blues. Porch ceiling
blue. Screen door blue. Toy chest
blue. Picnic table blue. Stair railing
blue. I've been collecting paint chips
like seashells in a small sand pail.
"Keep track of things," you'd said. "Write it
down. You won't remember all
those names, so many hues, forever."
O but I do. Mom would call you *Bob*.
Your mother always called you *Robert*.
And who, *Dad*—when you were just a tot—

would call you *Opie*? Your older sisters?
I wish I'd written down so much more.

Animal Stories

Barn Party, Vermont

Well, friends, here we are again.

How many heartbeats has it been
since we were last shepherded in
to the same shared space together?

Once, some years back,
one old friend was dumbstruck
to see inside this barn a spread
of fancy foods and guests in party
dress (a crowd that couldn't begin
to fill it up, from the stalls below
to the loft above). This farmer gasped,
and gawked, then squawked: "For God's sake—
put some animals in this place!"

Well, friends, here we are again.

We may not be a flock of sheep,
herd of cattle, or litter of pigs,
but haven't we all gladly sucked
our mothers' teats, laid down in grass,
peed in moonlight, or eaten scraps?

Maybe most stories of creatures
not just surviving but thriving—
outlasting storms and floating forward
into the future—owe a debt
to Noah and his well-wrought boat
(*and* to his wife, let's give *her* a line

and even say her name, *Naʹmah*).

Isn't there more to every story?

How this old barn is not a boat.
And we're not sailing over water.

But aren't we, all of us, afloat?
So how is it we stay buoyant?

Let's flesh the story out: Besides
the ark, and Noah the carpenter,
his helpmate, and the messenger
dove, let's not forget the animals
themselves, and the lessons of their living,
how they kept a lookout
for one another, pulled out splinters
with their teeth, licked each other's wounds,
groomed the fur and preened the feathers
of their fellow animal friends,
then snuggled side by side for warmth
through long stretches of chill and dark
and damp, and even cracked some jokes
to make each other laugh, and just kept on
keeping on, telling and
retelling their own animal stories
until the sun came out again.

En Plein Air

The plow draws furrows in contour lines
across the hillside from north to south

as yellow ochre umber leaves fall from trees,
curling downward like fine pencil shavings,

and Sun, lost in her own gradation studies,
lays down her graphite marks by deft degrees—

dark, then darker, darker still—until
her long thin shadows, from ridgeline trees,

have sown the fields with cross-hatched strokes
she's smudged from west to east at end of day,

highlighting her landscape in such enviable ways
the artist can only dream of mimicking one day.

Beekeeping

Once, we kept bees, in hives—
or, *they* kept *us*, kept us mesmerized,
kept us drunk on dandelions,
dazed and dizzy by roadsides,
kept us spellbound in fields
dusted in pollen, all abuzz,
kept us out in those downpours
in petals humming in orchards,
kept us fed on ambrosia,
appetites aroused—the bees, the bees
left us amazed under plum trees.

Some Curse, Some Sing

Some bristle. Some curse. Some call the sumac "evil."
Some slash its copse, curtail its crown, bedevil
and belittle it—come spring, come summer, come fall.

But winter's jay, she clears her throat—*Ahem*—she begs
to differ: She shakes her head, she's glad for dregs—
those ruby fruits she'll mine like gems amid the rimy tousle.
Some praise, some sing, give thanks, take wing. *Ave, Ave,*

Aves, some sing. Sing praise.
When jay swoops in—
                                        toolool, toolool—
she spies the juicy drupes. She seeks some sacred perch
and flaps her tired wing, she lights on hollow branch
then flaps her wings again. With bluest jay's descent
snow-crested boughs bow down, bounce right back up again
to spill their drifted mounds, reveal what had been hidden.
Ave, Ave, some praise, some sing.
                                        Ave Aves, take wing.

Some bristle, some curse, some call the sumac "evil,"
but winter's jay sweeps into view, an azure blur
on frosted air in search of hidden treasure—
all *queedle-queedle, toolool-toolool,*
                                        all noggin shake,
all plume and shimmy, all spirit quake, all set to slake
her thirst for sumac wine, to sip, to sup, and finally sate
her sumac berry hunger—but once she settles down to dine
jay always pauses first: She'll bow her feathery crested head
then lift her gladly open beak,
and in such random warbled keys she'll sing
her own *Hosannas,* in praise of ice-cold crumbs and all—

come spring, come summer, come fall.

                                                                        Some sing, some sing

come winter,
in praise—
                    O crimson spires!
in praise—
                    O sumac desire!

Shadows

Without a peep, deep from the yawning barn's ink-
black silhouette we seep, *un*-asleep. We spill
in silence in puddles in every shape of dark.
We curl up tight at your feet, then wake to pad
about all day, proverbial cats pacing the path—
mute as the marks beneath cat's practiced paws.

Notes from Woods Edge

      i

Bare knitting needles,
bright new skein, stitching Spring green—
leaf node leaf node leaf…

      ii

Watch how birds make nests,
make do with leftovers, take
shelter for others.

      iii

Birch bark scrolls uncurl
from trees so humbly swaying—
from trees so like us.

FIBONACCI BLUES

Blue

jay

swoops in,

then his twin,

now that's two who take

in crab apples as the crab tree

too takes in jay after jay, till three, then five—at last

count eight! Eight beaks grip, yank, pluck, then suck in winter's heady stock and in slaked succession

blue crests take off: jays in crescendo, flock after flock, winged integers ascending, snow motes descending, flake after flake, toward blue apogee

as temps drop low, breezes blow, jays lift, boughs bend, drift on drift, feathers flit, mischief trip, where are we now, blues riff, counting down, what are we up to, snow on snow, innumerably now— how much longer can this go up go down go on?

Orion

This evening's worn on. It's late
by the time Orion peeks from the alley
(after the bar, the band, the brawl,
the last call). He rises, he peers around,
he steps out further, he cinches his belt.
He stands proud. He swears,
                every so often moved
by a well-worn notch or two, *this*
is the one belt he's *always* worn—
forget his full belly bulging above—
since the days, seems just eons ago,
when he was young, a sparkle in your eye.

The Pleiades

Who? Oh, *those* sisters? They're everybody's
envy—their dance cards forever full.
It's as if they *invented* dancing.
They're the "it" girls, in gloss and glitter,
in sequined lace, but still demure.
No plunging cleavage, no blinding bling,
just hints of sex appeal through seven veils,
cascading hems, old-fashioned things.
Such an inseparable cluster they are,
constantly rising above sibling rivalry.
So much allure—for the Pleiades girls—
sparks from just how close they are.

Water Lily

You know, Mom, the water lilies are all
in bloom again, with their bright green leaves,
like big saucers, and their white blossoms, so
full, like porcelain tea bowls we'd use two hands
to hold if we could. Don't we wish we could
hold each other's hand? It's August already.
It's hard to know we won't be sipping tea
together, that you won't see Vermont this year.
Remember the cove beside the neighbor's dock,
where the north shore bends, where paper birch
and ash arch over the water, where you swam
that time, summers ago? I see you there
even when you're not. Like a favorite Polaroid
tucked safely away, bringing memories back
each time it's held again, the water lilies keep
popping into view, returning me to you, as if
you're here, buoyant among them, treading
water, your legs rippling the surface, pale lily
stems undulating, the lake water so clear,
your face a flower tipping toward the sun.

Cochlear

Regard
the wanting ear,
the dowager who tilts
her silver head nearer
the surgeon who considers
the elderly woman,
her dotage, her ear,
the moon—
all her phases—
how the moon
remaining whole
appears to wane,
how the woman
appearing whole
remains, does wane.

Sorrow Ghazal

for my sister and brothers

Forgive me. Mea culpa. Beg pardon. I'm so sorry—
It's a never-ending list, all the ways we say we're sorry.

Mom, I say, how about we don't say *sorry* today?
"What's that love? I can't hear you," she says, "I'm sorry—

I'll be right back. One sec. Let me get my hearing aid."
I rethink repeating myself. What's one more *sorry*?

Moving toward ninety now, my mother's begun to fail,
and as she leaves the room, I begin to feel sorrow.

I can hear her humming, but then: "Oh gosh," she sighs.
"Looks like my battery died." She's back with "I'm sorry,

sweetheart, my eyes aren't what they used to be.
Here, maybe you could help me? Again, I'm sorry.

Sorry to be such a bother. It's gotten so trying."
It's no trouble, Mom, really. It's me who's sorry

I can't help more. I can see what you mean, it is hard.
Here, try this. That should do it. Now, no more sorrys.

"Okay, thank you. You always were so good at fixing things.
Just like your father. Oh, there I go, forgive me. Sorry,

I do go on. I'll stop. I've just been missing him so."
I know. There, there, it's okay. Don't be sorry.

We hug each other tightly, and long.
If I could fix it all I would, I say, I'm sorry.

"You know, I can see your father still, in all his children.
It's too bad he can't see you now. Aren't we both sorry?"

Hourglass

O hourglass, is this where our Time begins, or where it stops?
When will we learn to tell the bottom from the top?
To see how the one side's full, the other's not?
These sands of time, grown dry, still weep,
grain after grain, always spilling away,
all at once and one by one—sifting,
shifting scales of time atilt—
another hour trickling...
on and on to meet
drip, drip, drip
its tipping
point
to
point
its tipping
drip, drip, drip
on and on to meet
another hour trickling—
shifting scales of time—atilt
all at once, and one by one sifting
grain after grain, always spilling away
these sands of time grown dry. Still, weep
to see how the one side's full, the other's not...
When will we learn to tell the bottom from the top?
O hourglass, is this where our Time begins or where it stops?

WATCHMAKER

Left behind, they gather dust. His collapsing
systems of mismatched cardboard shoeboxes,
the disconnected pieces—copper, brass, steel,
partial and whole watch and clock movements,
an unsettled mess of detached hands and faces,
the works gone mute, not ticking yet refusing
to be junked. In the back storeroom, an empty
cherrywood case, its disembodied balance,
dial, key, and chimes arranged and labeled,
even its pendulum buffed up a bit, now off
to one side, all there at his wooden workbench,
waiting. And inset in the antique mantle clock's
rehung door, a pair of small round windows
polished to shine like the sun and the moon: Viewed
through the top pane, roman numerals orbiting
clockwise from I to XII; and framed in the pane
beneath, a black-and-white etching, a bit like
Vermeer, mother and daughter standing on a floor
whose checkered tiles recede toward the garden's
back door, just as now, beyond this scene, so far
from this room, strangers in black lower by canvas
straps his gray casket into soil and flowers.

Out on the Lake in Our Old Canoe

in memory of my father,
on realizing this day in June falls on his birthday

You know, Dad, Leonard Cohen says *there's a crack*
in everything, sings *that's how the light gets in.* Looking
over the side of the canoe as I go, I squint in the sun and think
of how you taught me to steer a boat with different strokes,
and now each time I tickle the smooth face of the lake
with the sure J-stroke of my paddle, in its wake,
I swear, I can see giggles rising, the surface breaking
into a smile, a wink, even your dimples coming back.

Why I Still Write

Because on Monday I am not a Syrian refugee, fleeing
with nothing but my name, lost on a 2-year-long waiting
list to safety. Because Tuesday I am not the hawthorn tree

found feeble with rot in our yard, trunk collapsing to its core.
Because, come Wednesday, I'm neither my neighbor's lost curls
nor her wept tears, dropping onto the chemo chair.

Because these late-September temperatures never did plummet
as predicted by Thursday, and I can't forget to plunge again
into the piercing lake, to swim once more, deliriously numb.

Because on Friday morning, not another soul in my garden,
I work leaf litter into loss, kneading the earth while kneeling down,
grateful to have known the hawthorn—its blossom and its thorn.

Because we can't even fathom an age as old as Saturn's—
four-and-a-half billion years—yet already, before it's over,
we've begun to miss *this* day, the one we've just been given.

And the one after that. Because on Sunday, after nightfall,
we sit under dark skies on our wobbly outdoor lawn chairs,
their old joints creaking, the wood silvering to gray, all

of us waiting together—mother, father, and son-on-the-cusp-
of-adulthood—warm under blankets, the air grown cool,
our puppy roving from lap to lap, wondering what's up

as we speak or don't speak. In the welcome quiet, gazing
out across the lake, up over tree line, our heads tilted back,
we stare in awe at the Super Blood Moon, just now eclipsing.

Because, whatever Science says about some equal future moon, I know the rare particulars of this vast and intimate brilliance— the *now* of us—won't ever, in our lifetime, come my way again.

The Sea of Poetry

for Elizabeth Spires

"Lie gently and wide to the light-year
stars, lie back, and the sea will hold you."
—Philip Booth, from "First Lesson"

Its sparkle catches my eye. Can I, *may I*, go closer?
You stood nearby. I could hear your voice.

The breezes blew in, and whispered: *We're sweet. We're salt.*
The waves rolled in, and lessened, to not intimidate.

And then, the words you said to me: *Yes, you may.*
I tiptoed into the shallows. I wanted to stay.

Poetry lapped my toes. My bare soles tickled
as it trickled under, over, around. I wriggled

in that same spot, amazed. I was sinking in
as the *lap, lap, lapping* kept happening then.

Later on, I'm wading in, no deeper than my knees.
I splash and sing, remember nursery rhymes.

Soon, I'm in up to my waist. I can see over
small waves, can swim some, can stand and wave

to shore. I lie back and float, look up, let go,
take in sun and clouds, the sky—all it holds.

I bob up and down. I think how I'm held too.
Out here in the deep I am something to see.

I can touch the seafloor, bounce up, break free
and suddenly I've reached the buoy, the *me* I swam out to.

Sorting the Dark from the Light

Another cycle done.
Slow dancing down-cellar
to the hum of furnace
and washer, I'm folding
my arms as if around
my mother, cradling warmth,
her last nightgown pulled from
the unspinning dryer,
hem silently sweeping
the floor as we waltz, waltz…
1, 2, 3…
1, 2, 3…
as if she were as tall
as I, as if this space
I hold so dear were *her*—
beyond this perfumed air.
Isn't she here with me?
She must be here with me.
I know she's here with me.
We're waltzing, not weeping.
Stop weeping, we're waltzing.

♦

We pray and
we cry and
we sing and
we laugh
and
the hours
are spun of gold.

—M.F.E.

♦

Notes

The *stonechat* definition is from *Oxford Languages* online.

The grouse haiku was written by my father.

The Mary Ruefle quote is from an interview with her by Lisa Grgas, "On Grief and Gratitude: A Conversation with Mary Ruefle" in *The Adroit Journal* (October 24, 2019), and used with permission.

In the poem "*Reflection*," the repeated line "I have always loved the word *reflection*" was inspired by the first (and last) line of David St. John's poem "Guitar:" "I have always loved the word *guitar*."

Thanks to Elizabeth A. I. Powell for choosing an early version of "Diptych: Boathouse in Autumn Rain" for *GMR Online,* and for a remark that led me to recraft it into the two-part mirror poem included here. Gratitude as well to Bill and Catherine for writing time in a boathouse built for the muses.

"This Be the Oyster" exists only because of osmosis and what I've absorbed across years of slurping, seeing, and seafaring with Rowan Jacobsen.

"White Space & Ink" is an erasure from text in "The History of Relief," Chapter 1, in *Printmaking: History and Process* by Donald Saff and Deli Sacilotto from among my undergrad studio art books.

In the villanelle "On Waking," the line "Let the first thoughts of the morning be your own" is from a personal story told among friends by Jesse LoVasco.

"The Dream" is for my brother Gene who out of the blue sent me a postcard of Paul Gauguin's "Self-Portrait in Hat" with a sonnet of his own, inspired by that painting, on the back. I used his poem's last line, "I'm done with love, I think I'll take a nap," to begin "The Dream," a poem I then sent back to him on a postcard of Marc Chagall's painting of the same name.

"Birthdays Like Chanterelles in Golden Light" was written for Nancy on her 70th.

"Ode to Ceres and Her Golden Dome" owes so much to the caretaking of Vermont State Curator David Schütz, and to the beautiful and exacting work of artisan gilder Anne Domenech.

"Animal Stories" was written for Laura, with warmth for gatherings in our friends' 1888 Cummings Barn.

In the poem "Some Curse, Some Sing" the sounds for the blue jay calls ("queedle queedle" and "toolool") are from John Eastman's fabulous discussion on the behaviors of Blue Jay (*Cyanocita cristata*) in his book *Birds of Forest, Yard, and Thicket*, illustrated by Amelia Hansen.

A number of anaphoric and "why I write" poems and essays informed my "Why I Still Write," but hearing Major Jackson read his "Why I Write Poetry" at Bear Pond Books really woke it up for me.

The brief thread of words ending with "the hours are spun of gold" was written by my mother.

ACKNOWLEDGMENTS

Some poems in this book first appeared, sometimes in different versions, in the following print and online publications:

"Birthdays Like Chanterelles in Golden Light" in *Cold Mountain Review*; *The Singing Bowl*
"Blue" in *The Greensboro Review*
"Diptych: Boathouse in Autumn Rain" in *Green Mountains Review* (GMR Online)
"Child" in *Three Line Poetry*
"Cochlear" in *The Cincinnati Review*
"Come Home" in *One*
"Dragonfly" in *Four Way Review*
"The Dream" in *Literary North*, in "Constellation Ekphrasis"
"How a Sonnet Wakes Up" in *deLuge Journal*
"Ode to Ceres and Her Golden Dome" in *The Barre-Montpelier Times Argus*
"Orion" in *The Greensboro Review*
"The Pleiades" in *The Blue Mountain Review*
"Pondweed" in *SWIMM Every Day*
"The Red This Fall" in *American Journal of Poetry*
"Reflection" in *The Lyric* (winner of the Lyric Memorial Prize)
"Sleepwalker" in *deLuge Journal*
"Slice of Morning" in *One Art; Seven Days*
"Some Curse, Some Sing" in *The Remembered Arts Journal*
"Sponge Bath" in *storySouth*
"Squirrel" in *American Journal of Poetry*
"Stonechat" in *Southern Poetry Review* (winner of the North Carolina Writers Network contest)
"This Be the Oyster" in *The Greensboro Review*; *Poetry Daily*; *The Essential Oyster* by Rowan Jacobsen

"Watchmaker" in *The Greensboro Review*
"White Space & Ink" in *Literary North*, in "Constellation Seed"
"Why I Still Write" in *Paper Dragon*
"Wild in the Meadow" in *The Remembered Arts Journal*
"Wiping Dust from the *Atlas of Human Anatomy* in the Used Bookshop" in *The Decadent Review*

"On Waking" appears in the anthology *Birchsong, Poetry Centered in Vermont*, Vol. II, edited by Alice Wolf Gilborn (The Blueline Press, 2018).
From "Postcards from a Stack Tied Up with Twine," the first sonnet appears in the *PoemCity Anthology 2023*, compiled by the Kellogg-Hubbard Library (Rootstock Publishing, 2023).
From "Sponge Bath," part I appears in the anthology *The Path to Kindness: Poems of Connection and Joy*, edited by James Crews, Foreword by Danusha Laméris (Storey Publishing, 2022).
"Summer Cottage" appears in the anthology *How to Love the World: Poems of Gratitude and Hope*, edited by James Crews, Foreword by Ross Gay (Storey Publishing, 2021).
"Taking a Walk before My Son's 18th Birthday" appears in the anthology *Healing the Divide: Poems of Kindness and Connection*, edited by James Crews, Preface by Ted Kooser (Green Writers Press, 2019).

Gratitude

For the life behind these poems, I owe more than one debt of gratitude:

to my parents Robert & Maryan Elder, for raising their children with love, friendship, and the gift of "quiet time";

to my sibling chicks in the Elder nest whose company warms me—El, Gene, and Will, plus the one who happily flew in by marriage, Debbie—and to the memory of my youngest brother, David;

to my many writing workshop mentors—especially my first in poetry, Elizabeth Spires, and also David St. John, Peter Sacks, Alan Shapiro, Stuart Dischell, and Fred Chapell;

to all the insightful members of writing workshops in which I've ever taken part; and now, to FLOW (my four-lefts-one-write always-blooming writing group—JL, SS, LM, and AG);

to human and critter folks—chipmunks to my little brown bat—who've let me "say" my poems to them (with a few true-blue friends and one devoted dog topping the list);

to the places that have nourished my reading, writing, or practice of poetry—dirt roads & forest trails & paved streets & concrete sidewalks & shorelines & treasured water spots, fresh & salt both; and, for writing space when there seemingly was none, to the Vermont Studio Center for a Vermont Week (VTWK) residency; and to the Round Pond & Sterling Ridge writing retreats (CBK and LWM: How time flies!); to old wooden tables; to window seats; to libraries;

to Words Out Loud presenters and Art at the Kent creatives of all genres and mediums for their spark(s);

to anyone who's ever asked "Where can I get your book?" before there was a book;

to editors who've published my poems, with an extra bow to those who've done so more than once (Sue Scavo and Karla Van Vliet of *deLuge*; James Crews, editor of multiple anthologies; Elise Matich of *The Remembered Arts Journal*; Robert Nazarene of the *American Journal of Poetry*; a slew of *Greensboro Review* editors, in particular Terry Kennedy); and now, to Samantha Kolber of Rootstock Publishing (thank you Sam, for saying *Psst, over here*, and for your team's *abracadabra* of turning single poems into a collected whole that can be held);

to the woman who put her hand on her heart after attending a reading;

to EEJ, my one-and-only child-now-adult, who keeps mesmerizing me (plus: XOXO for the author photo!);

to Rowan, who one afternoon said *Hello* over a landline phone and told me what it was I wanted to do just then, to *not* do laundry but instead walk over and have wine on the porch in the rain with him; who has sheltered me under all manner of roof; who has walked with me through all sorts of weather.

About the Author

Mary Elder Jacobsen was born in Washington, DC, and grew up in Annapolis, Maryland. She holds a BA with honors in art from Goucher College, an MA from The Writing Seminars at Johns Hopkins University, where she was a teaching fellow, and an MFA in Creative Writing from the University of North Carolina at Greensboro. Her poems have appeared in various literary journals and have been selected for anthologies, radio, *Poetry Daily*, and other distinctions. A recipient of a Vermont Studio Center residency, she lives in North Calais, Vermont. *Stonechat* is her debut poetry collection.

More Titles in the Rootstock Poetry Series

Fire on a Circle by Kim Ward

Indigo Hours: Healing Haiku by Nancy Stone

Lifting Stones by Doug Stanfield

Mountain Offerings by Amy Allen

PoemCity Anthology 2023 by Kellogg-Hubbard Library

PoemCity Anthology 2024 by Kellogg-Hubbard Library

Safe as Lightning by Scudder H. Parker

The Lost Grip by Eva Zimet

To the Man in the Red Suit by Christina Fulton

Unleashed: Poems & Drawings by Betty Nadine Thomas

Poetry submissions are open. Learn more and submit at www.rootstockpublishing.com.

Milton Keynes UK
Ingram Content Group UK Ltd.
UKHW011840120424
441050UK00004B/223